FOLLOW US ON
INSTAGRAM
@KindergartenEducation

THIS NOTEBOOK BELONGS TO:

MORE BOOKS BY SMART KIDS NOTEBOOKS

(SCAN THE QR CODE OR VISIT: bit.ly/smartkidsnotebooks)

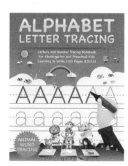

LET'S BEGIN BY RECAPPING THE LETTERS OF THE
ALPHABET

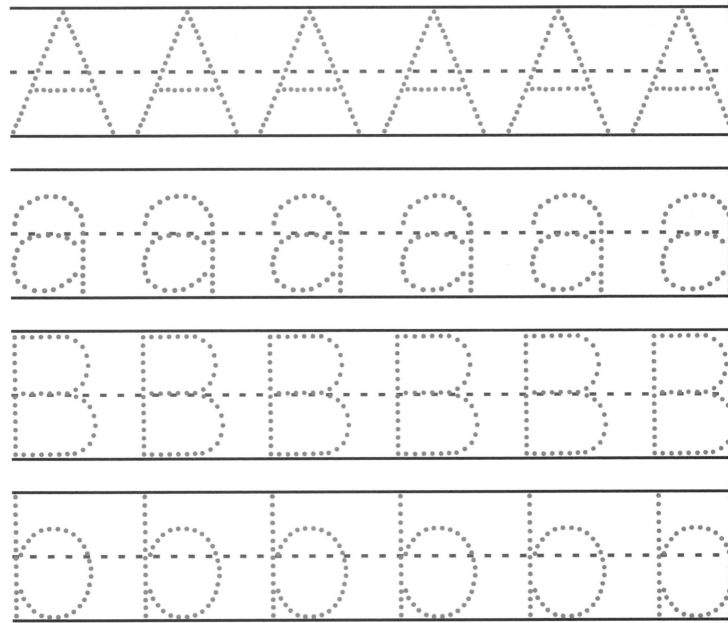

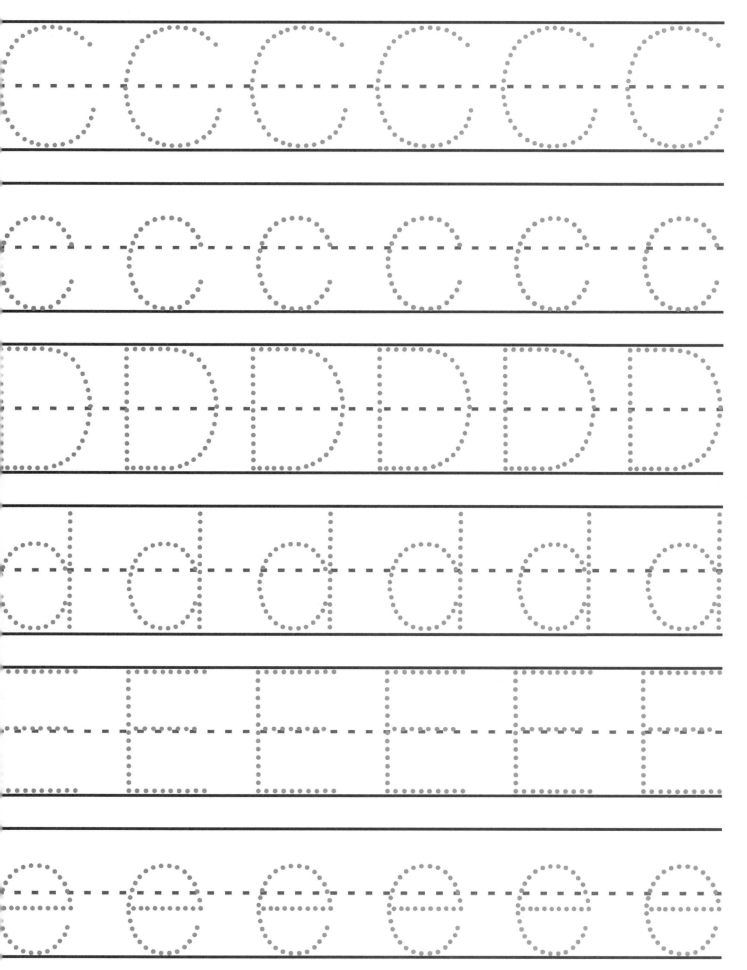

3

F F F F F F

f f f f f f

G G G G G G

g g g g g g

H H H H H H

h h h h h h

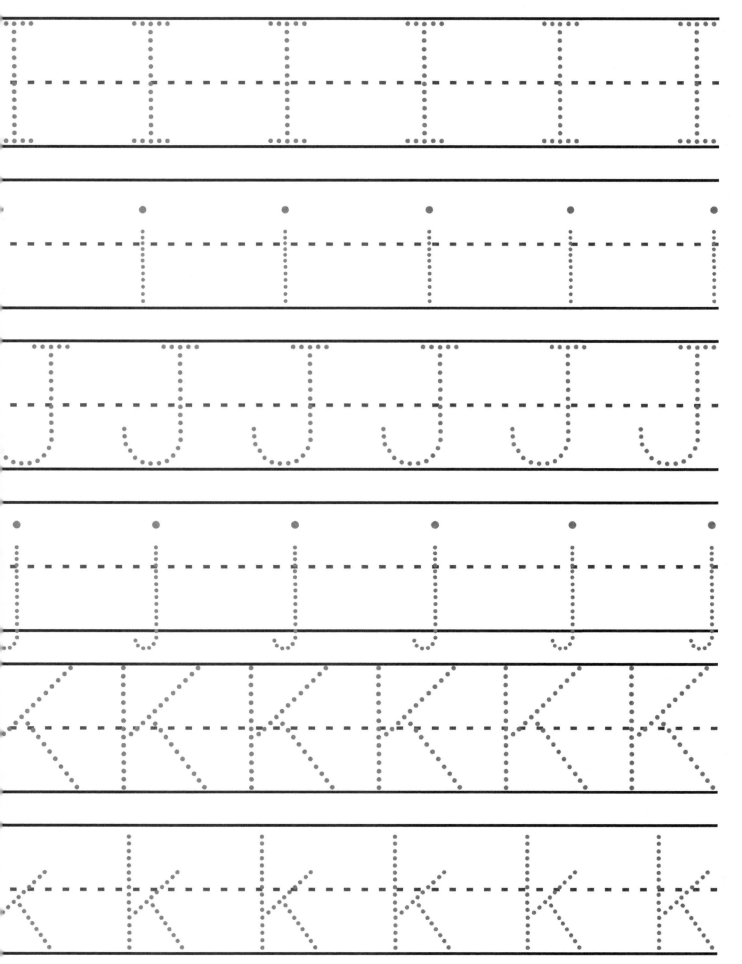

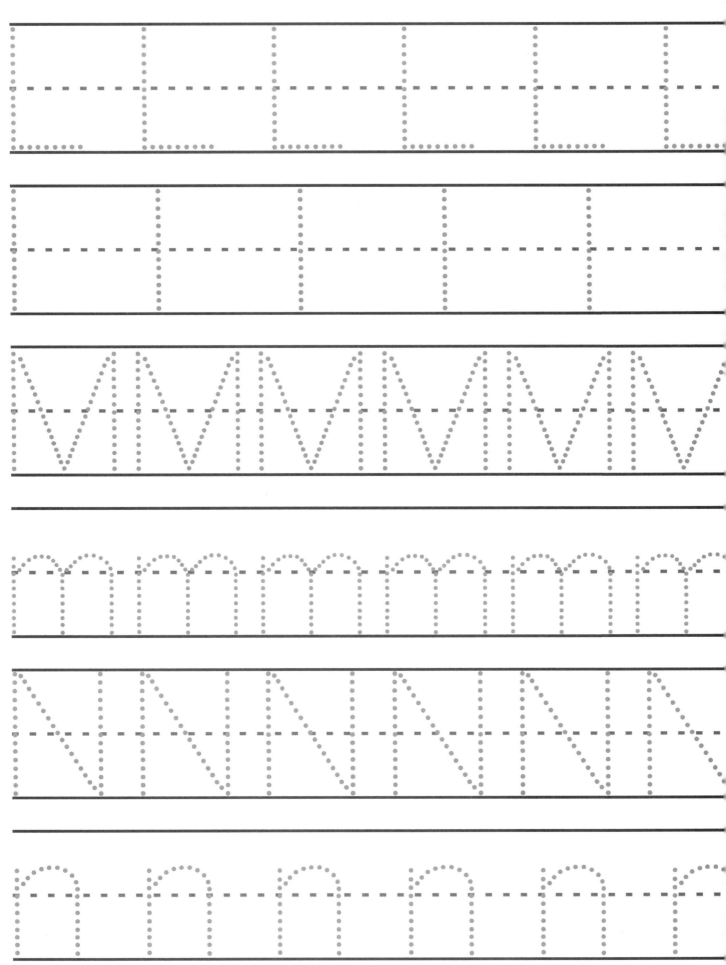

6

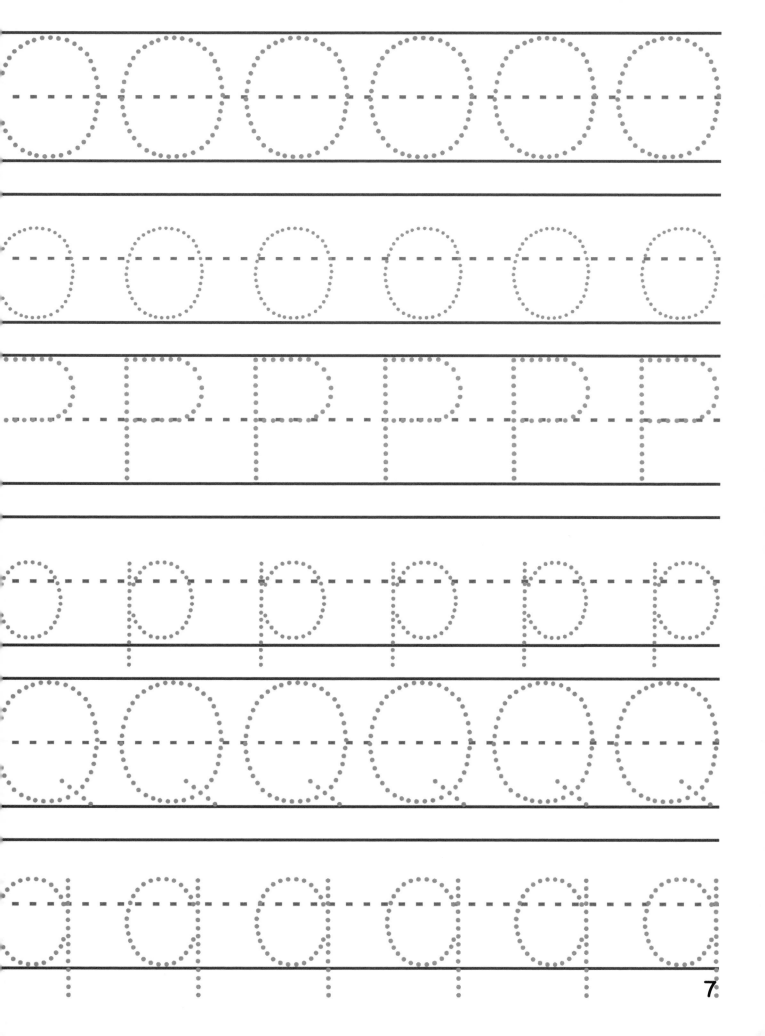

7

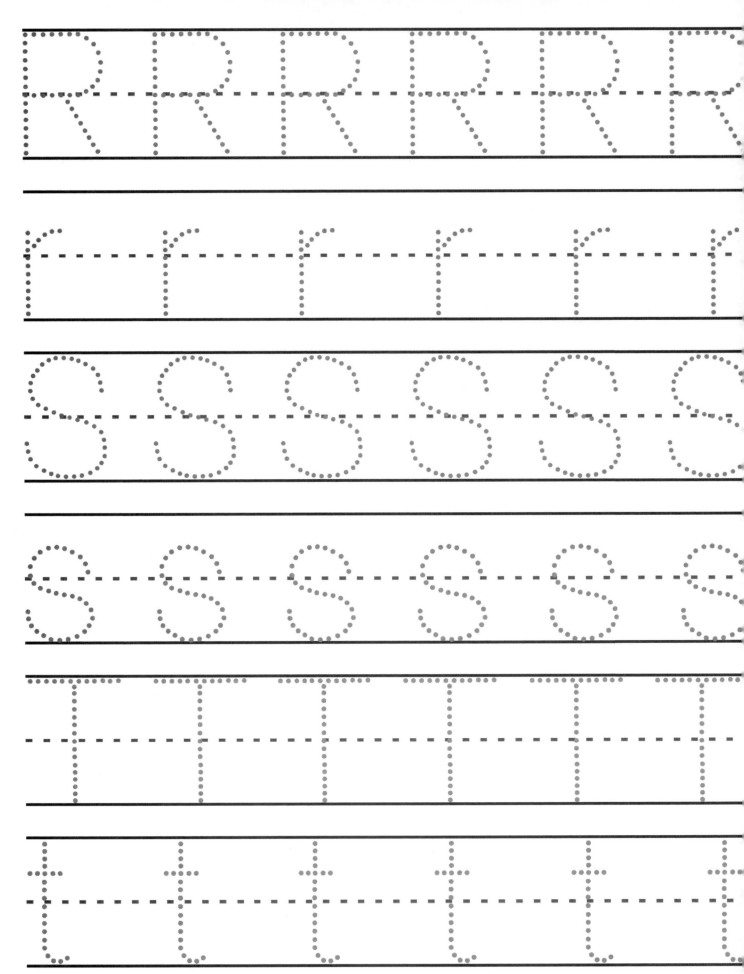

8

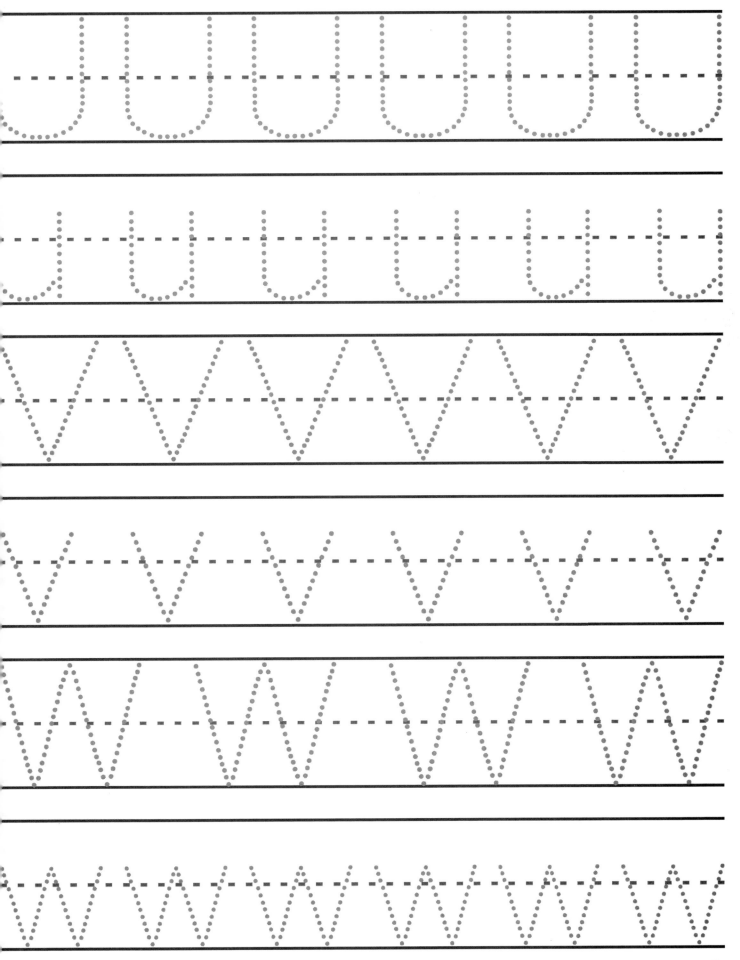

9

Table of Content - 200 Sight Words

I I am tall.

I I I I I I I I

I am tall.

am I am a good student.

am am am am am am

I am a good student.

you

Do you like veggies?

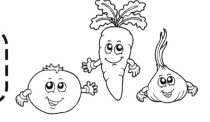

you you you you you

Do you like veggies?

are

There are many toys.

are are are are are

There are many toys.

she

She likes unicorns.

she she she she she

She likes unicorns.

the

I saw the bus.

the the the the the the

I saw the bus.

he   He likes fast cars.

he   he   he   he   he   he

He likes fast cars.

is   Their family is big.

is   is   is   is   is   is   is

Their family is big.

a — I saw a bear.

a a a a a a a

I saw a bear.

an — I saw an owl on the tree.

an an an an an an an

I saw an owl on the tree.

be

I will be home soon.

be be be be be be be

I will be home soon.

was

It was an interesting movie.

was was was was

It was an interesting movie.

have

Iguanas have tails.

have have have have

Iguanas have tails.

has

The deer has horns.

has has has has has

The deer has horns.

and

I like apples and pears.

and and and and and

I like apples and pears.

but

But I don't like tomatoes.

but but but but but

But I don't like tomatoes.

do

Do you like penguins?

do do do do do do

Do you like penguins?

did

Did you see the frog?

did did did did did

Did you see the frog?

we

We are in class.

we   we   we   we   we

We are in class.

they

They saw a ghost.

they they they they

They saw a ghost.

yes

Yes, I like oranges.

yes yes yes yes yes

Yes, I like oranges.

will

I will grow big.

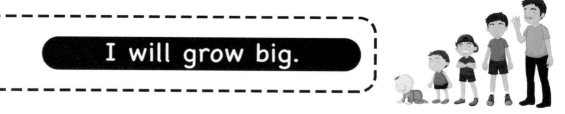

will will will will will

I will grow big.

22

no No pets are allowed here.

no no no no no no

No pets are allowed here.

not My backpack is not very big.

not not not not not

My backpack is not very big.

good   I am good at math.

good good good good

I am good at math.

well   I can swim well.

well well well well

I can swim well.

go   I go to kindergarten.

go   go   go   go   go   go

I go to kindergarten.

went   We went to my grandma.

went   went   went   went

We went to my grandma.

all
I ate all my lunch.

all all all all all all

I ate all my lunch.

at
I am good at writing.

at at at at at at at

I am good at writing.

any   I didn't see any whales.

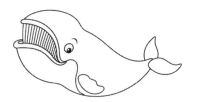

any any any any any

I didn't see any whales.

some   Can I have some chocolate?

some some some some

Can I have some chocolate?

can **Can you cook?**

can can can can can

Can you cook?

make **I can make pancakes.**

make make make make

I can make pancakes.

away — Keep away from fire.

away away away away

Keep away from fire.

out — I walked out of school.

out out out out out

I walked out of school.

for
The cake is for my friend.

for for for for for

The cake is for my friend.

get
We should get on the boat.

get get get get get

We should get on the boat

from   I got a doll from my mom.

from from from from from

I got a doll from my mom.

to   We walk to school.

to to to to to to to

We walk to school.

this This is a frog.

this this this this

This is a frog.

that That is a castle.

that that that that

That is a castle.

too

I washed my hands too.

too too too too too

I washed my hands too.

with

Can I play with you?

with with with with

Can I play with you?

up I wake up early.

up up up up up up up

I wake up early.

down They went down the slide.

down down down down

They went down the slide

on We saw a koala on the tree.

on on on on on on on

We saw a koala on the tree.

under Fish live under water.

under under under under

Fish live under water.

our
Our family went on a trip.

our our our our our

Our family went on a trip.

who
Who likes animals?

who who who who who

Who likes animals?

36

what **What color is your toy?**

what what what what

What color is your toy?

where **Where is my hat?**

where where where

Where is my hat?

here

I live here.

here here here here

I live here.

there

Put the toys over there.

there there there

Put the toys over there

in

They live in Europe.

in in in in in in in

They live in Europe.

into

Don't bring toys into the classroom.

into into into into into

Don't bring toys into the classroom.

it We like it here.

it it it it it it it it

We like it here.

so We are so happy.

so so so so so so so so

We are so happy.

me Unicorns make me happy.

me me me me me me me

Unicorns make me happy.

my This is my friend John.

my my my my my my my

This is my friend John.

big

Elephants are big.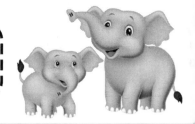

big big big big big

Elephants are big.

little

The mouse is little.

little little little little

The mouse is little.

42

like   I like playing outside.

ike like like like like

I like playing outside.

look   I will look in my room.

ook look look look

I will look in my room.

help

I will help you.

help help help help

I will help you.

now

We have Music now.

get get get get get

We have Music now.

must — You must finish the drawing.

must   must   must   must

You must finish the drawing.

please — Can I please go outside?

please   please   please

Can I please go outside?

find

I can't find my pen.

find find find find

I can't find my pen.

want

I want a cookie.

want want want want

I want a cookie.

live

We live in Canada.

live live live live live

We live in Canada.

pretty

My mom is pretty.

pretty pretty pretty pretty

My mom is pretty.

funny

Tell me a funny joke.

funny   funny   funny

Tell me a funny joke.

play

I like to play with you.

play play play play

I like to play with you.

jump

Rabbits can jump.

jump jump jump jump

Rabbits can jump.

walk

Turtles walk slowly.

walk walk walk walk

Turtles walk slowly.

new
He got new glasses.

new new new new new

He got new glasses.

soon
I will see my grandma soon.

soon soon soon soon

I will see my grandma soon

see Eagles can see very well.

see see see see see

Eagles can see very well.

saw I saw the moon.

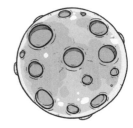

saw saw saw saw saw

I saw the moon.

run

I can run fast.

run run run run run

I can run fast.

ran

He ran to the doctor.

ran ran ran ran ran

He ran to the doctor.

say

Parrots can say words.

say say say say say

Parrots can say words.

said

He said a joke.

said said said said

He said a joke.

fly

We will fly on a plane.

fly fly fly fly fly

We will fly on a plane.

ride

I can ride a horse.

ride ride ride ride

I can ride a horse.

come
Lions come from Africa.

come come come come

Lions come from Africa.

came
The dog came to me.

came came came came

The dog came to me.

eat

I like to eat ice cream.

eat eat eat eat eat

I like to eat ice cream

ate

I ate all the pizza.

ate ate ate ate ate

I ate all the pizza.

black

The cat is black.

black　　　black　　　black

The cat is black.

white

Polar bears are white.

white　　　white　　　white

Polar bears are white.

brown

The wood is brown.

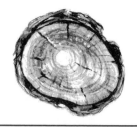

brown   brown   brown

The wood is brown.

yellow

The sun is yellow.

yellow   yellow   yellow

The sun is yellow.

blue

The blue whale is big.

blue   blue   blue   blue

The blue whale is big.

red

Roses are red.

red red red red red

Roses are red.

one
I see one police car.

one one one one one

I see one police car.

two
I have two coins.

two two two two two

I have two coins.

60

three
I see three birds.

three   three   three

I see three birds.

four
I have four fish.

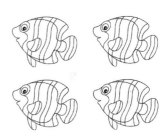

four   four   four   four

I have four fish.

five — I have five books.

five five five five five

I have five books.

six — There are six kids here.

six six six six six six

There are six kids here

seven · I am seven years old.

seven   seven   seven

I am seven years old.

eight · Spiders have eight legs.

eight eight eight eight

Spiders have eight legs.

nine

I wake up at nine.

nine   nine   nine   nine

I wake up at nine.

ten

I have ten fingers.

ten   ten   ten   ten   ten

I have ten fingers.

ask

I will ask my teacher.

ask ask ask ask ask

I will ask my teacher.

let

Let me sing.

let let let let let

Let me sing.

very The tree is very tall.

very very very very

The tree is very tall.

much How much do you weigh?

much much much much

How much do you weigh?

them — The map belongs to them.

them them them them

The map belongs to them.

us — Read us a story.

us us us us us us us

Read us a story.

as I am as fast as a flash.

as as as as as as as

I am as fast as a flash.

by I sit by the window.

by by by by by by

I sit by the window.

about I learned about Easter.

about   about   about

I learned about Easter.

got He got a new fish.

got got got got got

He got a new fish.

after
Eat your veggies after school.

after   after   after

Eat your veggies after school.

again
I saw a spider again.

again   again   again

I saw a spider again.

70

first
I made my first cookies.

first first first first

I made my first cookies.

best
She is the best player.

best best best best

She is the best player.

these
These cookies are mine.

these these these

These cookies are mine.

those
Put those books here.

those those those

Put those books here.

which — Which is faster?

which   which   which

Which is faster?

would — Would you like a pear?

would   would   would

Would you like a pear?

73

why — Why are you scared?

why why why why why

Why are you scared?

because — I like school because it is fun.

because because because

I like school because it is fun.

work

Finish your work.

work work work work

Finish your work.

done

I am done training.

done done done done

I am done training.

try

I will try to read.

try try try try try

I will try to read.

use

You can use my spoon.

use use use use use

You can use my spoon.

their

Their house is big.

their their their their

Their house is big.

your

I saw your car.

your your your your

I saw your car.

thank | Thank you for the cake.

thank   thank   thank

Thank you for the cake

think | I think I am sick.

think think think think

I think I am sick.

78

call

I will call my family.

call call call call call

I will call my family.

before

Come home before five.

before before before

Come home before five.

both We both went for a walk.

both both both both

We both went for a walk

many How many cats do you have?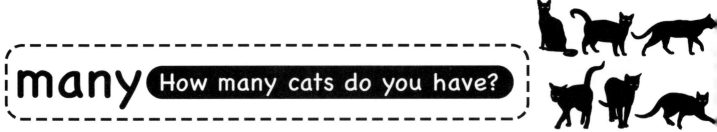

many many many many

How many cats do you have?

bring

I will bring my notebook.

bring bring bring bring

I will bring my notebook.

keep

Keep the keys.

keep keep keep keep

Keep the keys.

clean

Clean the table.

clean clean clean clear

Clean the table.

cut

Cut the paper.

cut cut cut cut cut

Cut the paper.

cold

The ice is cold.

cold   cold   cold   cold

The ice is cold.

warm

The tea is warm.

warm   warm   warm

The tea is warm.

could | I wish I could swim.

could could could could

I wish I could swim.

been | The weather has been rainy.

been been been been

The weather has been rainy

does   Does she play piano?

does does does does

Does she play piano?

don't   I don't like cherries.

don't don't don't don't

I don't like cherries.

draw

We like to draw.

draw draw draw draw

We like to draw.

drink

I like to drink juice.

drink drink drink drink

I like to drink juice.

every   I like every animal.

every   every   every

I like every animal.

always   I always wash my hands.

always   always   always

I always wash my hands.

fast

Cheetahs are very fast.

fast fast fast fast

Cheetahs are very fast

sleep

Bears sleep all winter.

sleep sleep sleep sleep

Bears sleep all winter.

found

I found my toy.

found found found

I found my toy.

made

I made a mess.

made made made made

I made a mess.

give

Give me my scarf.

give   give   give   give

Give me my scarf.

gave

She gave me a hug.

gave   gave   gave   gave

She gave me a hug.

90

going   I am going to eat.

going going going going

I am going to eat.

goes   She goes to school.

goes goes goes goes

She goes to school.

had I had a dream.

had had had had

I had a dream.

his I like his bike.

his his his his his

I like his bike.

her
That is her doll.

her her her her her

That is her doll.

him
I saw him reading.

him him him him him

I saw him reading.

how

Show me how to jump.

how how how how

Show me how to jump.

know

I know how to dance.

know know know know

I know how to dance.

its

The skunk lifts its tail.

its its its its its

The skunk lifts its tail.

or

Do you like cats or dogs?

or or or or or or

Do you like cats or dogs?

just

I just got home.

just   just   just   just

I just got home.

once

I visited the zoo once.

once   once   once   once

I visited the zoo once.

may — I may go to the beach.

may   may   may   may

I may go to the beach.

were — The apples were sweet.

were were were were

The apples were sweet.

never   `I've never been to Paris.`

never   never   never

I've never been to Paris

today   `Today is a sunny day.`

today   today   today

Today is a sunny day.

of

The chair is made of wood.

of of of of of of of of of of of

The chair is made of wood.

off

Turn off the TV.

off off off off off

Turn off the TV.

old My grandma is very old.

old old old old old

My grandma is very old.

grow Apples grow on trees.

grow grow grow grow

Apples grow on trees.

open
Open the door, please.

open open open open

Open the door, please.

over
Summer is over.

over over over over

Summer is over.

own — I can write on my own.

own own own own own

I can write on my own.

small — Hamsters are small.

small small small small

Hamsters are small.

pull
The horse will pull the cart.

pull pull pull pull pull

The horse will pull the cart.

full
The box is full of photos.

full full full full full

The box is full of photos.

put

Put the toys in the box.

put put put put put

Put the toys in the box.

take

I will take my glasses.

take take take take

I will take my glasses.

read I like to read books.

read read read read

I like to read books.

write I will write my homework.

write write write

I will write my homework.

wash

I will wash the dishes.

wash wash wash wash

I will wash the dishes.

wish

I wish to go home.

wish wish wish wish

I wish to go home.

right
That is the right answer.

right right right right

That is the right answer.

sit
Please sit down.

sit sit sit sit sit sit

Please sit down.

round — The ball is round.

round   round   round

The ball is round.

around — I walk around my house.

around around around

I walk around my house.

sing

Let's sing a song.

sing sing sing sing sing

Let's sing a song.

tell

Tell me a joke.

tell tell tell tell tell tell

Tell me a joke.

stop

I am at the bus stop.

stop stop stop stop

I am at the bus stop.

show

I will show you my cat.

show show show show

I will show you my cat

then I will sleep and then go out.

then then then then

I will sleep and then go out.

when When are we leaving?

when when when when

When are we leaving?

FOLLOW US ON INSTAGRAM
@KindergartenEducation
to have a chance to win FREE notebooks

EXPLORE MORE OF OUR EDUCATIONAL NOTEBOOKS ON AMAZON